How I Lost My Virginity

A sad story of how my little sister was raped to stupor

Ellen Richardson

Contents

CHAPTER ONE

I forever thought-about myself to be a typical adolescent, however wanting back, I'll have qualified as a touch of a "nerd", for lack of a higher term. I ne'er extremely had a drag with lecturers, and as a result, ne'er had to check all that onerous, or that a lot of. At the ripe adulthood of seventeen, and in my last year of high school, I ought to have had the globe by the balls. For the foremost half, I did, too, apart from one little, insignificant detail. I had a sister that was a year younger than i used to be. Now, which may not seem to be a giant downside, and for the foremost half, it wasn't. Except that this specific sister was associate degree absolute knock-out, in my mind.

I was born on the primary of November. My pa forever same that he and mum had been out trick-or-treating, and that i was the treat. My Mom, on the opposite hand, patterned that i used to be a unclean, rotten trick that somebody had compete. to the current day, she still believes that. Anyway, my sister, Joanne, was born the subsequent Sep, and she or he was forever Mom's "little baby". The title wont to drive Jo completely crazy, however I'd use it if I required to urge her attention. She'd typically retaliate with one thing like associate degree object that was each shut at hand, and appropriate to be used as a fatal projectile. As you'll tell, we have a tendency to had USual|the standard|the same old} relation group action happening between us.

But it wasn't all cats-and-dogs fights. Despite the actual fact that we have a tendency to had our battles, we have a tendency to had our sensible times, too. If i used to be feeling down and out, Jo was forever there, attempting to cheer ME up. Whenever it absolutely was her that was on the outs, I felt compelled to do and be there for her. At the time, I had no plan of why, however I forever perceived to fret for her happiness and welfare. therefore once Jo knocked on my room door one evening, getting into before I might say a word, I might tell by the frightened look on her face that one thing in her very little world wasn't quite right. At the time, i used to be a touch upset at the approach she simply interjected, however wanting back, i'd have granted her access while not hesitation, and my permission wasn't extremely necessary.

"Jim, am i able to discuss with you?" she nearly voiceless. That look on her face created it nearly not possible to refuse her request. Even at sixteen, she knew a way to push my buttons, which unhappy expression, those rimmed eyes from crying, all found simply the proper heart-strings to pluck.

"Sure, Sis," I conceded, "any time, you recognize that. You appear as if you simply lost your ally. What's up?"

Joanne simply stood there, watching the ground, apparently attempting to seek out simply the proper words, and having no success whatever. I got up and walked over to her, wrapping my arms round her and pull her to ME tightly, then kissed her forehead. She would possibly solely be my sister, however she was a really special person in my life, and therefore the sight of her pain ripped an enormous chunk out of my heart. Finally, she found the bravery to appear into my eyes, and that i might see that she was deathly petrified of one thing.

"Okay, I offer up" I relieved into her house. "Something's got my sister all twisted and out of form. {are|ar|area unit|square MEasure} you gonna tell me regarding it, or do I actually have to play twenty questions?" I had another line that I typically used, however this wasn't the time for it. within the time it took Joanne to finally get the words out, I might have created another half-dozen gap lines, all of them new and untested.

"Jim, am I a . . . lesbian?" she squeaked. you may have detected a pin drop, even on the opposite facet of city. however the hell was I presupposed to answer that one? Hell, however was I presupposed to even perceive her question?

"Okay, Jo, I offer up" I sputtered. "I'm a guy, and guys browse newspapers, not minds. What the hell ar you talking about?" i used to be somewhere between being terribly confused, and feeling just like the stupidest person on the earth.

"Jim, I'm scared!" she nearly screamed at ME, then regathered her cmposure. "I was over a Sarah's last night, and that we were . . . well . . . playing around, you know? Anyway, Sarah got some booze from her previous man's liquor cupboard, and that we got a touch drunk. Somewhere on the road, we have a tendency to started talking regarding . . . sex, among alternative things. She asked ME if I'd ever kissed somebody, you know, on the lips? therefore I told her the reality, no. Suddenly, she leaned over and kissed me! Not simply a touch peck, either, however a full-blown, open mouth, tongue swapping, buss. At first, i used to be appalled, however the longer she kissed ME, the a lot of i started to relish it. consecutive issue I knew, i used to be smooching her back!"

"Umm, I don't suppose one kiss would qualify you as a lesbian, Jo" I advanced associate degree opinion. "The booze may need had one thing to try and do with it, and with the approach it felt." the design on her face told ME that my reassurances hadn't done a damned little bit of sensible.

CHAPTER TWO

"It . . . it wasn't only 1 kiss, Jim. there have been countless them. we have a tendency to should have kissed for pretty much associate degree hour. Then Sarah grabbed my boob, and started to squeeze it, twiddling with my . . . my nipple, too. And you recognize what? I favored it!"

I took the time to let her words sink in. Hell, she was sixteen, and doubtless as interested by sex as i used to be, and perhaps a lot of therefore. however like ME, i used to be pretty positive that she was still a virgin, which might justify why a kiss would spark her interest. the actual fact that it absolutely was from one among her girlfriends was a touch exhausting to grasp for a man like ME, but then, I wasn't all that knowledgeable on however a girl's mind worked.

"There's a lot of, isn't there?" I quietly asked. the design in her eye told ME that those kisses were simply the start.

"Yeah, there is" Jo continuing. "When she grabbed my boob, and started to play with it, I did identical to her, and it felt therefore tremendous. I simply knew a way to bit her, to excite her, to convey her identical reasonably pleasure she was giving ME. we have a tendency to unbroken on smooching, and twiddling with every other's tits.

Jim, I couldn't stop! I simply wished to feel her boobs, and the way exhausting her nipples got! Pretty before long, we have a tendency to were on the ground, and Sarah lay on high of ME, pull my shirt and my brassiere off, then taking hers off similarly. once she mashed her tits against mine, i believed i'd die, it felt therefore good!"

Joanne took a deep breath, rental it out slowly before occurring, as if to bolster her bravery. Then she looked deep into my eyes, and if I had any queries on her muliebrity, they disappeared in this one second. She should have found that bravery she required, as a result of she went on together with her tale.

"Jim, Sarah reached down between my legs, and started to rub ME down there, and it felt completely fabulous! I followed her lead, and therefore the next issue I knew, we have a tendency to were each naked, touching and feeling one another, and that i couldn't get enough of her fingers tickling or teasing me! Sarah was therefore wet, and then slippery. I favored that texture of her sex. She began to finger ME, and that i thought i used to be progressing to explode, it felt therefore heavenly! I wished to try and do identical to her, to form her pussy feel pretty much as good as she did mine. Then Sarah should have had associate degree sexual climax, or one thing, as a result of she began to moan and groan, and that i felt her shaking and unsteady. At first, I didn't recognize what was happening to her, however she force ME tighter to her, then shoved herself down on my fingers and created positive I couldn't pull them out. God, she should have cask like that for over a moment. once she was done, she started twiddling with ME some a lot of, and therefore the next issue I knew, my pussy was tingling, my tummy got all fluttery, and that i felt like i used to be losing management of myself! and therefore the shivery part? I simply didn't care! no matter was happening to ME, I wished it a lot of and more! i suppose i have to have gotten those self same shakes that Sarah got, as a result of all I will bear in mind is that I felt like somebody had zapped ME with electricity. My head was swimming with what sounded like bright lights! Al I might think about was that I wished Sarah to stay doing no matter it absolutely was she was doing to me!"

At that time, Joanne born her gaze from my eyes, and started to stare at the ground once more. All this point, I'd been holding her by the shoulders, however I had a burning need to carry her tightly in my arms. As I did, the tip of her nose rested against my Adam's apple, and that i kissed her forehead once more, holding my lips to her in an endeavor to inform her that everything would be alright. it's going to are a pipe-dream, however I had to do. Then another time, I force back simply enough to appear into her eyes.

"Sis, it looks like you 2 had your 1st orgasms. Not being a woman, I'm solely guess, however it positive looks like it. That's an honest issue, in this currently you recognize what to expect. however I doubt that creates you a lesbian." I had to raise her consecutive question, if for no alternative reason than to assist calm her fears. "Sis, am i able to raise you one thing personal?" I waited for her response.

Jo found at ME, unsure whether or not or not she wished to open herself up that a lot of to her brother, however she enclosed exhausting, then nodded her affirmation.

"Have you ever been with a guy? I mean . . . well, you recognize what I mean. have you ever let a man into your pants yet?" I got a convincing smack for my bother, and it hurt like thunder, though i feel a great deal of it absolutely was the shock of my sister truly placing ME, quite the impact of her hand on my face.

"Oww!" I screamed. "What was that for? Shit, I asked you if it absolutely was okay, and that i told you it absolutely was personal. You didn't got to smack ME like that!"

"Whether I actually have or not is none of your fucking business!" she snapped. "And only for your data, no, I haven't!"

"Okay, okay! however you didn't got to smack ME. it's going to not be any of my business, and it extremely doesn't concern ME, personally. Hell, it's your body, and you'll provides it to anyone you are feeling snug with, for all I care. however I had a reason for asking, and it positive as fuck wasn't to be snoopy, or nasty. So, will we have a tendency to strive that once more, while not the slapping and hitting?"

My sister looked into my face, and that i might see her sorrow staring back at ME. She leaned up and kissed ME gently on the jaw bone, then force ME tight to her young adolescent body, nearly as an indication of desperation for the protection of someone's embrace.

"I'm . . . I'm sorry, Jim. I shouldn't have done that, however your question simply created ME furious for a second there. i suppose I lost it. Forgive me?"

"Umm, shouldn't have done what, Sis? ill-treated ME, or kissed me?" it absolutely was an endeavor to interrupt the strain, and it should have worked, as a result of my sister truly began to smile, for the primary time since she'd walked into my space. That smile created it fully unessential to answer with words, and that i kissed her forehead an added time.

"Jo, if you haven't had sex with a man, however the hell ar you presupposed to recognize what you want? therefore you and Sarah had sex along. therefore what? It's most likely no massive deal, and I'll bet she's feeling as unnecessarily guilty as you, right now. And I'll additionally venture that you simply 2 aren't the sole ladies to experiment with another lady, either. however till you've had sex with a man, don't trouble labelling yourself as straight, lesbian, or perhaps bisexual! you have got no approach of knowing till you have got all the knowledge . . . and at once, you don't!"

Joanne stared at ME for the longest time, her very little mind whirring with thoughts and schemes. I might hear the gears going around, and a few of the teeth weren't lining up quite properly, I swear. She had one thing devious that she was plotting, that I knew by the expression on her face.

"There's a technique to seek out out, Jim" she same softly. "You and that i might get it on . . . couldn't we?"

"Jo! What the fuck ar you talking about? I'm your brother! That's wrong, and you recognize it!" I nearly screamed at the highest of my lungs. And yet, her plan got caught within the cobwebs of my mind. My sister positive wouldn't qualify because the ugliest lady within the world, that's evidently. Okay, perhaps she wasn't as developed as a number of her friends. Even at sixteen, she was still solely associate degree A-cup. She'd asked ME, many times before, once she'd finally get larger boobs. i attempted to chalk it up to her being a late bloomer, and had forever assured her that in the future, her bust would fill out. In purpose of truth, it ne'er did, and even nowadays, many decades later, she's still associate degree A-cup. On her, though, it's sensible.

"Besides," I went on, "Mom and pa ar home. If we have a tendency to got caught, there'd be hell to pay, associate degreed you recognize it!" it absolutely was an excuse, and a reasonably flimsy one, at that. She still had the prettiest face I'd ever seen, a lean and trim body, if somewhat flat-chested, soft and delicate curves to her waist and back resolute her aesthetic hips, then right down to a distinguished butt that projected out from the little of her back, slowly returning to those firm thighs that topped her legs. and people legs! Of her five-foot-four-inch height, I generally swore that the primary four feet were leg! God, they were gorgeous!

"Are you spoken language that you simply wouldn't wish to own sex with ME, massive brother?" she threw in my face, knowing what the important answer would be. I'd got to be a castrate to not get turned on by her body! however she was my sister, for God's sake! And nevertheless . . . and yet . . . .

"Oh, for Christ's sake, Joanne. That's cheating, and you fucking-well recognize it!" I knotted in exasperation. "You recognize damned well that if I ever had the possibility to form like to you, I'd grab it. however we have a tendency to can't tonight, and by tomorrow, you'll have modified your mind . . . right?" She continuing to appear at ME therewith conniving stare, going ME guess at what her answer may be.

"No, I don't suppose therefore, Jim," she finally declared, "unless you don't wish to. If mum and pa weren't right downstairs, I'd get it on with you during a heartbeat, to be honest. you'll be my massive brother, and it's going to be wrong, however you've forever turned ME on, in your own, sweet way. But, if you actually don't wish to . . . "

The turmoil in my head was nearly dangerous enough to require associate degree salicylate for. Here I was, reproval one among the prettiest ladies I'd ever met, her desirous to get into my pants – there's a switch! – and that i was choking as a result of what? as a result of she was my sister, for crying out loud!

CHAPTER THREE

Somewhere within the cosmos, there's presupposed to be some reasonably God that appears down on U.S., making an attempt to guide and nurture U.S.. I don't recognize if any of that's true, however if it's, he's a sadistic son-of-a-bitch, in my opinion! And right then, he was most likely riant his guts out, knowing however badly he had ME squirming! I might think about quite an few names to decision him, and most of them went through my head, missing my vocal chords by mere fractions of an in.. 'Fuck you', I thought.

"Okay, simply supposing we have a tendency to did undergo with it, Sis. wherever does one propose we have a tendency to make out, and when? Tonight's out, obviously, however what regarding tomorrow, when school? Mom's operating till four, therefore she won't be home before 5, and pa ne'er gets home a lot of before six."

Shit, i used to be extremely grasping at straws here, however the thought of being with Joanne, feeling her soft and sleek skin, her warmth, her femininity? There was no approach I might pass that probability up! perhaps the thrill and taboo of criminal congress was another driving issue, however it felt thrilling as hell to suppose about!

"Okay, tomorrow, when faculty, then" Jo volunteered. "Do you would like {to MEet|to satisfy|to fulfill} me here, or ought to we have a tendency to walk home together? we have a tendency to don't, usually, and Sarah would possibly get a touch suspicious if we have a tendency to do. however I'd find it irresistible if we have a tendency to did walk along, if for no alternative reason than I relish being with my massive brother, sometimes" she advised.

"Yeah, which may be reasonably neat, walking home with you. however why not walk with Sarah, too? we have a tendency to simply won't let her recognize that we're progressing to be . . . you know. nobody would suspect a issue if

Sarah was with U.S. . . . would they?" I threw in. we have a tendency to mentioned some minor details, however finally in agreement that we'd all walk along on the approach home, and check out to form it seem to be a coincidence that Joanne and that i happened to air identical street at identical time. That was another detail we have a tendency to had to orchestrate, however my sister perceived to suppose she had it taken care of.

The next day, it absolutely was all I might consider, this liaison between my sister and that i. The day perceived to drag, and my thoughts were all over however on my school assignment. Even my instructor snapped my set off for creating numerous mistakes at school, and I'm sensible at maths. Our lunch break was solely associate degree hour, however it felt sort of a week. I unbroken wanting round the eating house, attempting oceanrch out} Joanne during a sea of 4 thousand alternative students, however with no luck. it absolutely was most likely for the higher that I didn't, for I'd have had no plan what to try and do if I did notice her.

Joanne had organized it in order that she and Sarah would simply happen to be by the outside door as I came out, then she'd decision resolute ME, and we'd go from there. i attempted to act casual, and to the current day, I still suppose I ought to have won associate degree accolade for my performance. however we have a tendency to did manage to tug off our casual meeting at the facet of the college, walking and talking like we have a tendency to generally did, whenever it became necessary to form the trip along. That was one thing that happened throughout snowy weather, but today, the sun was out, the grass was inexperienced, and it absolutely was pleasantly heat. Oh well, I thought, shut enough for what Jo and that i had in mind. Yeah, right!

Most of the talking was between Sarah and Joanne, with ME eavesdropping sort of a snoopy brother, and keeping my massive mouth shut. I don't suppose Sarah even knew i used to be there, 0.5 the time. She unbroken commenting on this boy, or that person, speculating on whether or not they were fascinated by her or not. I knew the answers, however I wasn't close to deflate her ego with the reality. My gut instinct was that Sarah urgently wished to urge arranged , and she or he didn't appear significantly fussy regarding WHO took her cherry.

If she'd solely identified what Joanne and that i were close to get into, she'd have wet her panties!

Finally, and that i do mean finally, we have a tendency to came across the house, and Sarah same her good-byes for what sounded like a month, then eventually turned and left for her own house. i used to be therefore tempted to run up the steps and thru the outside door, however that might have broken the illusion. we have a tendency to sauntered up and into the house. As before long as that door closed, though, the illusion was now not necessary, and that we positive didn't waste any time. I had simply enough time to hold my coat up and take away my shoes before my sister threw her arms around ME and force ME to her hungry lips. Somewhere within the method, I born my books, touch my toe, however ne'er felt a damned issue.

Instantly, my sister became the Alpha and Omega of my aware world. Her lips tasted therefore damned sensible, and once her tongue began to trace across my lips, i'd have danced on hot coals for a lot of of her kisses. She demanded that I grant her access to my mouth, and that i volitionally given. Oh God, might that lady ever kiss, too! She ran an exploration over my higher teeth, flicking the tip on my high palette, then running over each surface of my tongue. Her passion sent shivers up and down my spine, and that i control her to ME as tightly as I dared, nearly as if i used to be afraid that this was all a dream, and that i would possibly awaken. we have a tendency to should have stood simply within the outside door, kissing, for fifteen minutes or a lot of. By then, my blood was no quite one or 2 degrees off the boiling purpose.

"Still interested?" Joanne quizzed ME. I kissed her an added time back, and she or he molten in my arms. As we have a tendency to finally poor our lip-lock, she nearly ran up the steps, then stopped at the highest landing, looking forward to ME to each catch up, and to point that of our 2 rooms I most well-liked. I selected my very own, just because that's wherever I patterned we'd be the foremost snug. As before long as I radio-controlled her into the space and closed the door, Joanne force her fill up, then turned to ME with simply her white brassiere covering her underdeveloped breasts, and beckoned ME to her once more. As i started to kiss her soft, sweet lips, my hands migrated to her diminutive mammaries, pressing and squeeze her deliciously pliable skin through the material of her brassiere, revelling within the sensation of her nipples growing tougher, and sticking themselves into my waiting palms.

Without rental my lips return loose, Joanne moaned at the eye to her breasts, pressing them tighter to my hands. She had ME unfree there, creating it not possible to succeed in behind her and undo the clasp. In frustration, I merely hooked my fingers within the midriff adornment, and force it out and up, exposing her little however definitive young breasts to my curious explorations. As I ran my fingers over her currently rock-hard nipples, she moaned a touch louder and a touch longer, whereas still looking each nook and cranny of my mouth together with her tongue. If she had force my head any tighter to her, I might have simply nibbled the rear of her neck whereas still barred to her lips. Eventually, I had to return up for air, as Joanne reluctantly free her death grip on my head.

"Oh God, Sis," I moaned as my lungs finally crammed to capability, "you style therefore damned sensible, and feel even better!"

"You like my very little tits, Jim? They aren't a lot of, however you create them feel therefore good! ar you defeated that they're therefore small?" For that one moment, being lost in Dolly Parton's cleavage would are a let-down, compared to the wondrous joy of being allowed to pleasure my sister's breasts. I answered taciturnly, my lips finding and capturing one among her teats as I continuing to stroke and tweak the opposite. She nearly hummed as she moaned in grateful delight, and that i might feel the same sound forming within ME, too.

As I continuing to please within the style, texture, and openness of her miniature mammaries, i started to steer her backwards towards the bed. The backs of her knees contacted the bed, and she or he flopped onto it, her back landing on the softest a part of the pad, with ME still clamped to her sex organ. I braced my fall with my alternative hand simply enough to stay from landing on her, however unbroken on suction and teasing her tit. I'm unsure if she relinquished her hold on my head, however if she did, i used to be saved in seconds. But again, I had to return up for air.

"You feel a great deal higher than Sarah" Joanne cooed. "God, does one ever!"

I began to kiss my approach down her tight very little belly, intrigued with the feel of the within of her navel on my tongue. Jo giggled a touch, most likely as a result of she found my explorations tickling, however uncontrollable. As I continuing down towards her crotch, I undid her pants, then relieved them and her panties down and off her satiny, sleek legs. My sister lay there, clad solely during a non-functional brassiere, and therefore the sight nearly created ME choke with lustful wish. My nose was assailed with the scent of her sex, which very little blond patch of hair simply on top of her mound intrigued the hell out of ME. I buried my nose in it and indrawn deeply. By then, the attract of her slit had snagged my full attention, and that i simply had to explore its line of work.

My tongue fell down over her gash, feeling her outer lips parting gently as they yielded to ME. I knew one thing of a woman's physiology, largely from the sex books I'd browse, along side the written pornography that every one young males appear to gravitate towards. i used to be sorting out quickly, though, that there was a massive distinction between the word and therefore the actual wonders of the feminine body. I'd detected of a clit, however had ne'er seen one in real world, and that i simply had to seek out Joanne's. Easing my tongue into the highest of her slit, I detected that tiny bump that work the outline I'd examine, and started to flick the tip of my tongue over it. 2 things happened, nearly at the same time. Joanne's clitoris began to stand up to my tongue and become exhausting, and that i got my 1st intoxicating style of feminine juices. There was a 3rd reaction, too, as my sister indrawn sharply, then clamped her hands on my head and pushed ME tight to her pussy. I licked, lapped, and lathered her slit, fascinated by the engorging of her knotting stub, obtaining drunk on the style of her juices, and drawn to the parting of her outer lips as I continuing to stimulate her female genitalia. As I fell any between her thighs, my tongue found her heavenly entrance. it absolutely was then that I 1st touched and tasted her barely-protruding inner lips. I had ne'er seen a woman's duct up shut like this, and that i upraised my head simply enough to urge an honest read of her entryway to paradise. Those slowly rising inner lips waved gently like line of work ME to them. I ran the tip of my tongue between her inner and outer lips, beginning at very cheap of 1 facet, circling and flicking against her clitoris, then returning to her alternative 2 lips. Feeling brave, i attempted inserting my fat tongue into her duct, and was rewarded with Joanne breathing sharply yet again, followed at once by a lustful groan from her luscious lips, those on her face. additionally to her sounds of delight, i used to be given another deposit of her heavenly juices, that I lapped up sort of a sottish sailor with a freshly opened bottle of rum.

'Oh God, Jim!" Joanne moaned softly. "I don't recognize what you're doing, however it feels therefore fucking good! Keep going, massive brother, please!" she demanded, and that i was excited to be ready to offer her that sort of delight. As I unbroken imbrication up and down her slit, Joanne began to rock her hips, still pressing my head tightly into her pussy, her legs currently unfold as wide as she might get them, and bent at the knee. in this position, her ass cheeks were in-tuned with the bed, however each legs were suspended within the air. I continuing, and she or he affected those legs in order that they rested on my shoulders. Suddenly she flung her head back, inflicting her pelvis to push up against my lips. I might hear her respiratory amendment, changing into a lot of insistent as she took shorter however deeper gasps. Then, unexpectedly, my sister began to twitch her hips, the movements changing into a lot of and a lot of pronounced, and therefore the next issue I knew, she was shaking and trembling violently, still forcing ME tightly to her crotch. As if all that weren't enough for a teen that had ne'er practiced a lady in sexual climax, Joanne began to howl, softly initially, then louder and a lot of forcefully. Soon, she was bucking sort of a mad stampede rider. i used to be unable to help stapled against her quivering pussy, nearly missing the flooding of my face together with her juices. however with the primary style, I furiously slurped and defeated all i used to be given, driving my poor sister deeper and deeper into her climax. She should have seed for a full 2 minutes.

Finally reposeful when her sexual climax, Joanne force ME from that fountain of nectar, pried her eyelids open enough to check ME, and given ME with a glance of absolute joyous rapture. I felt privileged to own been allowed to convey her that, however wasn't quite ready for what she same next.

"Where the fuck did you learn to try and do that? Christ, i believed i used to be progressing to lose my mind, for a moment there! that point with Sarah was particular, however what you simply did to ME was . . . unbelievable! that ladies have you ever been with?"

CHAPTER FOUR

"Actually, Sis, you're the primary lady I've ever defeated down there. I got the concept from one among those girlie magazines, and thought I'd strive it. Glad I did, too, as a result of you style extremely great" I answered her.

"What the hell do they decision that one?" Joanne demanded.

"I suppose they decision it ingestion pussy, or one thing like that," I answered her, "but there's a clinical name for it that I can't pronounce. All i do know is that i really like it, and it doesn't appear to interrupt your heart either. It felt such as you had one hell of associate degree sexual climax out of it. Am I right?" She nodded her head within the affirmative. "I like to feel you going off like that," I same softly, "so perhaps we should always try this again?"

"Oh yeah," Joanne responded sky-high, "any time you want! Even Sarah doesn't understand that one, and I'll be damned if I'm progressing to tell her. Besides, however the hell would I justify my massive brother ingestion my pussy to Sarah? Hmm?" I felt a passing wave of panic, as I pictured the commotion of Sarah's inquisition. however I knew that our secret was safe with Joanne, if for no alternative reason than she was as liable as i used to be.

"Umm, Jim?" Joanne poor into my reverie. "Do you continue to wish to try and do it with me? Go all the approach, I mean?" I felt like telling her it absolutely was regarding the stupidest question she might raise. At this time, i'd have even thought-about forcing myself on her, though deep in my soul, I knew I wouldn't truly make out.

"Yes, Sis, I do, if you continue to do," I moaned softly, "but given that you continue to do."

"Get those pants off, and let ME see it. I've ne'er seen a boy's exhausting cock, therefore this may be another 1st on behalf of me, won't it?" my sister nearly ordered ME. I stood up, undid my pants, then pushed them and my briefs to the ground. Joanne's eyes were rivetted to my throbbing member because it twitched and danced in anticipation. the actual fact that she was observing my exhausting cock was one issue, and I'll admit that it absolutely was a thrill to show myself to her. however that glassy look of lustful marvel can stay graven in my memory for the remainder of my life. She sat up, watching my up-curved erection with curious marvel, then found into my eyes with a silent plea in her eyes. I replied by poke my hips forward ever slightly, and she or he reach out, wrapping her hand around my shaft. As she slowly fell her fingers down from the pinnacle to the bottom, then make a copy, her gaze shifted from my member to my face, reflective her questions on a man's erect member.

"Oh Jim, it's therefore exhausting, and nevertheless therefore soft" she murmured. " I simply love the texture of it in my hand! I actually have this urge to slip my hands up and down it. might I?" she begged. There wasn't a lot of probability of ME spoken language no, and that i nodded my head, giving her full permission. She began to explore this new a part of her increasing world, slippy softly and sensuously up and down my shaft, her fingers causation waves of electric-like pleasure in the course of my groin. As she reached the tip once more, there was a glance of curiosity in her eye. She fell her fingers through the little pool of pre-cum that had gathered there, smiling gratefully at the satiny texture of the liquid lubricating substance.

"Is that your semen?" she asked with some apprehension.

"No, that's pre-cum, Sis," I explained, "sort of like your pussy juices. It's there to lubricate each folks in order that once it goes in your . . . " I couldn't decide what label to decision my sister's duct, and visually pleaded for her to bail my sorry ass out.

"My cunt?" Joanne equipped.

"Yeah. once it goes in your cunt, it'll slide right in while not pain you. perhaps it's a secondary issue, however maybe not all ladies get as slick as you're, right now" I finished. whereas still holding my cock in her hand, Joanne fell her finger down her slit, and that i saw the tip of it disappear into her entrance. The sight nearly created ME seed right there. She fell it in and out of her canal one or two of times before wanting make a copy at ME, then whereas still gazing in my eyes, began to finger herself once more, her eyes changing into glassy and unfocused.

"I don't suppose there's a lot of probability of binding within ME, right now" she moaned softly. "My cunt's soaking wet, particularly when you Greek deity ME like that." Then she came her attention to my throbbing manhood captured in her fingers, look herself stroke ME, whereas still pumping her own finger in and out of her cunt. Suddenly, she affected her stare back to my eyes.

"I wish to feel it within ME, Jim" she growled. "I wish to grasp what looks like to own a man in my cunt. return and place it in me?"

As I leaned forward, Joanne flopped back on the bed, her legs still unfold wide, and her face showing the breathless anticipation of giving herself for the primary time to any man. I prayed that I'd be all she ever hoped for, and perhaps a touch a lot of. I relieved myself between her thighs, and she or he radio-controlled my cock to her entrance. I felt the resistance of her gap, not nevertheless distended enough to require the pinnacle of my cock into her. Applying associate degree oscillatory pressure against her labia lips, I felt her inner ones flap slightly against the tip of ME, finally yielding as my cockhead popped into her waiting love canal. I'm unsure that one among U.S. was deeper in sensual shock, Joanne, or me.

"Oh my God, Jim! That feels . . . awesome!" I relieved a touch a lot of of my manhood into her slowly, and as I did, my sister gasped at the thrilling realization that she was being penetrated by a person for the primary time in her young life. Not solely was she close to be fucked, however she nearly perceived to be impatient for it to happen.

I began to push myself deeper within Joanne, nearly surprised at the warmth that her sex radiated, and captivated by the slippery tightness of her duct, it's satiny walls causation a exacting need in ME to plunge wildly into her depths. The slight friction of her lining on the ridge of my helmet perceived to beckon and decision ME to increase myself absolutely within her, nevertheless I went at a leisurely pace, lost within the delirious sensibility of my 1st coupling. Then I saw her maidenhead's barrier, and felt my sister wince because the resistance stopped my progress.

"Ouch!" she moaned. "I forgot that. You're progressing to got to bust my cherry, Jim, as a result of i would like to feel all of your cock within ME. i would like to feel it's full length filling ME up. God, you have got no plan however sensible this feels!"

"It's progressing to hurt, I think, Sis" I warned her. "Are you positive you would like to travel through with this, or would you rather stop? Once your hymen is broken, we are able to ne'er return once more."

Joanne stared at ME with wide eyes, that look of determination broadcasting itself deep into my soul.

"Yes, massive brother, i would like this. i want to feel you all the approach within ME. i want to grasp . . . if I'm a lesbian or not. We'll ne'er conclude unless you are doing this on behalf of me. Please, massive brother? Please?" she begged. I couldn't refuse her, not for love nor cash, however at identical time, i used to be quite simply a touch apprehensive regarding what she was progressing to undergo, and therefore the associated pain that I'd got to cause her. That half I didn't notice too thrilling.

With all the tenderness I might muster, I fell my arms up beside her, holding her shoulders with my hands, attempting urgently to let her recognize that i used to be compassionate what she was close to expertise, and praying that I might build it alright for her. Then I had a concept, and leaned forward enough to kiss her soft, pouty lips. whereas her attention was momentarily pleased, I force myself back simply enough to convey my cockhead space to create up some momentum, then quickly drove my cock through her barrier, finally ending up with the tip simply resting against her cervix.

"Holy Shit!" Joanne screamed. "God dammit, that hurts!" she howled.

"We will stop, if it's an excessive amount of, Sis. I can't handle the concept of inflicting you pain. i feel it's as a result of i really like you too damned much" I confessed.

"No!" She was insistent currently. "Just let ME get wont to losing my cherry. i would like this, Jim, therefore bad! I style of knew that my 1st time would hurt, however i want to grasp . . . whether or not i'm or not. currently that we've gone this way, i would like it all." She reached up and force ME to her lips once more, smooching ME exhausting and long, as if that kiss would build the pain get away. Then, unexpectedly, Joanne began to carefully rock her hips, slippy her cunt up and down atiny low portion of my cock.

"Oh God, y-e-e-s-s-s!" she growled. "Fuck me, Jim! build ME a woman! build my cunt tingle find it irresistible did once you Greek deity ME out!"

Tentatively, I withdrew myself till solely my cockhead remained, then i started to ease my manhood into the depths of her newly-deflowered womanhood. With every stroke, Joanne rocked her hips in syncopation, bit by bit increasing the tempo of our rhythm, till we have a tendency to were pounding against one another sort of a number of rutting animals. I might feel the walls of her duct flutter, then her muscles began to grip and relax on my shaft, and as we have a tendency to continuing to fuck, those flagellations became a lot of and a lot of pronounced.

"Oh God, Jim! It's happening again! I'm progressing to . . . ", and therewith she began to gasp sharply in shallow bursts, which quivering of her hips grew into a series of trembling shakes as she vibrated to a lower place ME. inside many fast strokes, Joanne began to cry, her sounds slowly increasing till it became a coffee scream, building in tone and amplitude sort of a symphonic crescendo. She proclaimed the arrival of her pleasure peak with a series of high-pitched grunted screams, her arms holding ME nearly tight enough to suffocate ME. I unbroken pumping myself into her, doing everything I might think about to stay her on the cusp of that wave of enjoyment that she rode.

CHAPTER FIVE

As Joanne began to ease down from her unleash, I might feel my balls begin to raise, and therefore the pressure at the bottom of my cock build, as that mass of creamy seed ready to unleash itself for the journey deep into my sister's female internal reproductive organ.

"Oh God, Sis! I'm progressing to cum!" I wailed.

"Yes!" she hissed deliriously. "Do it, Jim! seed within ME. i would like to feel you fill ME with liquid body substance and sperm! i would like to grasp what it's wish to be full of a man's essence!" I might feel that 1st stream of spunk hunting up my shaft, then explode from my hole, spraying deep into my sister's love chamber, gushing because it passed her cervix and into her womb! Then another, and another, and even another blast of my boiling baby batter percolated out of ME, change of integrity the primary strings because it unfold itself deep in my sister's lower belly. She had somehow managed to wrap her legs over my waist, and was pull ME deeper and deeper within her, and that i detected her lustful moan of enjoyment as she kissed and defeated my ear.

"Oh! My! God! Jim!" she gutturally growled I my ear. "I will feel it! I feel your seed within me! therefore good! Y-e-e-s-s-s!"

another time, I might feel her twitch, however while not the explosion of a full sexual climax to accompany it. As I felt the last of my seed ooze from my cock, i started to relax my finite muscles, and rolled over onto my back, clasping and holding my sister in order that we would stay united.

With the post-coital glow, my cock began to melt, then finally flopped out of Joanne's cunt, permitting a stream of our mingled juices to break of her, over my balls, and down the crack of my ass. during a little approach, it felt just like the similar to the flow of champagne once a bottle is 1st uncorked. I favored the texture of it, the feel of it, the implications of it. I wasn't too keen on the exciting odour, though. Suddenly, my space reeked of the smell of sex. Actually, it wasn't the smell, per se, that involved ME, however rather the possibility that somebody apart from the 2 folks would trespass into our non-public world, and conceive to destroy each it, and us. except for the instant, i used to be lost in this tremendous afterglow, and as long as Jo was there too, the remainder of the globe didn't MEan a damned issue to me.

"Oh God, Jim! That was . . . that was the foremost tremendous, stunning issue I've ever practiced in my whole life!" Joanne purred softly in my ear. "I've forever thought you were a really special guy, but now, I know it, inside in my heart. Would you be pained if I told you i really like you? That i feel I'm gaga with you, too?"

I kissed the sting of her ear, the sole a part of her that my lips would reach, as I confessed to her, "No, I wouldn't be pained, Sis. I'd be downright worthy.. once did you have got in mind to form this announcement? before long, I hope", and that i couldn't facilitate however giggle softly as I titillated this lady that had given herself to ME, her massive brother, and allowed ME to accompany her thereon journey to changing into an entire lady.

"Shut up, Jim, or I'll got to hurt you, you dumb shit!" Joanne growled softly at ME. "But if you're progressing to be associate degree asshole regarding it, I love you, massive brother, and I'm gaga with you, too!"

"Phew!" I voiceless back, "because I'm gaga with you, Joanne. i suppose I can't decision you a touch baby any longer, though, can I?"

"Not if you would like to measure long enough to check your eighteenth birthday, you can't!" she warned ME, then captured my lips an added time, whilst she scarf what was left of my heart.

"Oh, by the way, " she adscititious, "I've return to the conclusion that I'm undoubtedly not a lesbian. Feeling a man within ME is far higher than something Sarah might do on behalf of me, particularly once that guy is you."

I was progressing to say one thing like "I told you so", however I didn't have the bravery. Still don't, only for the record. I've seen my sister fight, and I'm too young to die.

THE END